Books

Like Clean Hands

KNOCK-KNOCKS,
Limericks and Other Silly Sayings

compiled by
Sandra K. Ziegler

illustrated by
Diana L. Magnuson
created by The Child's World

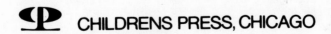 **CHILDRENS PRESS, CHICAGO**

Library of Congress Cataloging in Publication Data

Ziegler, Sandra, 1938-
   Knock-knocks, limericks, and other silly sayings.

   (Laughing matters)
   Summary: A collection of knock-knock jokes, sayings,
and rhymes such as: "Latin is a dead tongue, dead as it
can be. First it killed the Romans, now it's killing me."
   1. Wit and humor, Juvenile. [1. Knock-knock jokes.
2. Jokes. 3. Nonsense verses. 4. Limericks]
I. Magnuson, Diana, ill. II. Title. III. Series.
PN6231.K55Z53   1983   818'.5402'08   82-19764
ISBN 0-516-01872-8

TABLE OF CONTENTS

Where Did They Come From?

Knock-knock jokes are fun to tell and fun to make up. But how did they come about?

Way back in the 1920 and '30s, there was a period of American history known as Prohibition. During Prohibition, it was not legal to operate a tavern or sell alcoholic drinks—all liquor was prohibited (forbidden by law).

However, some people did sell alcohol in illegal restaurants called "speak-easys." To get into one of these places, people had to know its secret location and its operator.

At the door of a speak-easy, a patron would knock twice. The operator would ask, "Who's there?" And the patron would identify himself. It was because of this procedure that knock-knock jokes were born!

Knock-knock.
  Who's there?
Ima.
  Ima who?
Ima tired of knocking. Let me in!

Knock-knock.
  Who's there?
Elsie.
  Elsie who?
Elsie you later, alligator.

Knock-knock.
  Who's there?
Noah.
  Noah who?
Noah good place to
  swim?

Knock-knock.
  Who's there?
Rabbit.
  Rabbit who?
Rabbit up neatly. It's a birthday gift.

Knock-knock.
  Who's there?
Dishes.
  Dishes who?
Dishes the FBI.
  Open up!

Knock-knock.
  Who's there?
Isador.
  Isador who?
Isador open?

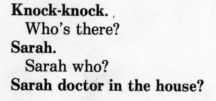

Knock-knock.
  Who's there?
Duane.
  Duane who?
Duane the tub. I'm dwowning!

Knock-knock.
  Who's there?
Sarah.
  Sarah who?
Sarah doctor in the house?

Knock-knock.
  Who's there?
Oswald.
  Oswald who?
Oswald my bubble gum.

Knock-knock.
  Who's there?
Hugo.
  Hugo who?
Hugo your way and I'll go mine.

Knock-knock.
  Who's there?
Ida.
  Ida who?
If Ida known you were coming, Ida baked a cake.

Knock-knock.
  Who's there?
Little old lady.
  Little old lady who?
I didn't know you could yodel.

Knock-knock.
  Who's there?
Alaska.
  Alaska who?
Alaska my mommy.

Knock-knock.
  Who's there?
Peking.
  Peking who?
**I'm going to wrap presents, and it's no fair
  Peking.**

Knock-knock.
  Who's there?
Cablegram.
  Cablegram who?
Cablegram if you find Grandpa's will.

Knock-knock.
  Who's there?
Robin.
  Robin who?
Robin banks will get you in trouble.

Knock-knock.
  Who's there?
Missouri.
  Missouri who?
Missouri loves company.

Knock-knock.
  Who's there?
Germany.
  Germany who?
Germany Cricket.

Knock-knock.
  Who's there?
Europe.
  Europe who?
Europe to no good.

Knock-knock.
  Who's there?
Veal.
  Veal who?
Veal my head and see if I have a fever.

Knock-knock.
Who's there?
Daryl.
Daryl who?
Daryl come a time when you need me!

Knock-knock.
Who's there?
Distress.
Distress who?
My mother made distress.

Knock-knock.
Who's there?
Anita.
Anita who?
**Anita umbrella
when it rains.**

Knock-knock.
Who's there?
Juneau?
Juneau who?
Juneau the way to go home?

Knock-knock.
Who's there?
Euripides (you-rippa-deez).
Euripides who?
Euripides shorts and I'll spank you!

Knock-knock.
Who's there?
Mickey.
Mickey who?
I tried to get in the house but mickey wouldn't work.

Knock-knock.
Who's there?
Isabel.
Isabel who?
Isabel going to ring soon?

Knock-knock.
Who's there?
Butter.
Butter who?
Butter late than never.

Knock-knock.
Who's there?
Jamaica.
Jamaica who?
Jamaica kite for the contest?

Knock-knock.
Who's there?
Nida.
Nida who?
I can never find my mom when I nida.

Knock-knock.
  Who's there?
Eileen.
  Eileen who?
Eileen when I climb up
  a mountain.

Knock-knock.
  Who's there?
Leaf.
  Leaf who?
Leaf me alone.

Knock-knock.
  Who's there?
Orange.
  Orange who?
Orange you glad it's Friday?

Knock-knock.
  Who's there?
Aida.
  Aida who?
Aida lot of cake and now my stomach aches.

Knock-knock.
  Who's there?
Harold.
  Harold who?
Harold are you? I'm eight.

Knock-knock.
  Who's there?
Handsome.
  Handsome who?
Handsome candy to me.

Knock-knock.
  Who's there?
Datsun.
  Datsun who?
**Datsun of mine is
  always into something!**

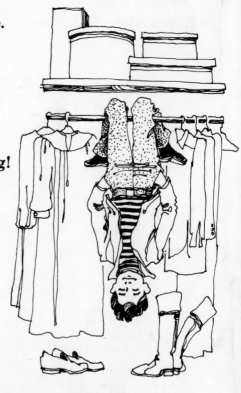

Knock-knock.
  Who's there?
Ammonia.
  Ammonia who?
Ammonia little boy.

Knock-knock.
  Who's there?
Baldwin.
  Baldwin who?
The bride baldwin the groom backed out.

Knock-knock.
  Who's there?
Cantaloupe.
  Cantaloupe who?
Cantaloupe; I'm already married.

Knock-knock.
  Who's there?
Boo.
  Boo who?
Don't cry; you'll be well soon.

Knock-knock.
  Who's there?
Freddy.
  Freddy who?
Freddy or not, here I come.

Knock-knock.
  Who's there?
Eddie.
  Eddie who?
Eddie body home?

Knock-knock.
  Who's there?
Gillette.
  Gillette who?
Gillette the cat out?

Knock-knock.
  Who's there?
Nomad.
  Nomad who?
I nomad at you; can't we be friends?

Knock-knock.
   Who's there?
Alfred.
   Alfred who?
Alfred the needle if you'll sew the button on.

Knock-knock.
   Who's there?
Letter.
   Letter who?
Letter in. It's raining outside!

Knock-knock.
   Who's there?
Arthur.
   Arthur who?
Arthur 'mometer says it's hot today.

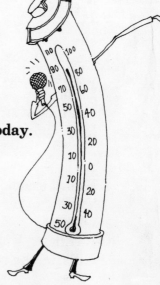

Knock-knock.
   Who's there?
Venice.
   Venice who?
Venice your papa coming?

Knock-knock.
   Who's there?
Olga.
   Olga who?
Olga away if you don't let me in.

Knock-knock.
  Who's there?
Hurricane.
  Hurricane who?
**Grandma wants to go for a walk; will you get
  hurricane?**

Knock-knock.
  Who's there?
Scold.
  Scold who?
Scold outside.

Knock-knock.
  Who's there?
Athena.
  Athena who?
Athena flying saucer!

Knock-knock.
  Who's there?
Swarm.
  Swarm who?
'Swarm and my ice cream is melting.

Knock-knock.
  Who's there?
Needle.
  Needle who?
Needle little time to make up my mind.

Knock-knock.
  Who's there?
Douglas.
  Douglas who?
Douglas in the dishwasher is dirty.

Knock-knock.
  Who's there?
Cheese.
  Cheese who?
Cheese a cute puppy.

Knock-knock.
  Who's there?
Butternut.
  Butternut who?
Butternut play with a toad or you might get warts!

Knock-knock.
  Who's there?
Thea.
  Thea who?
Gotta run—thea tomorrow.

Knock-knock.
  Who's there?
Vitamin.
  Vitamin who?
If that's Ed at the door, vitamin.

Knock-knock.
  Who's there?
Diploma.
  Diploma who?
**If the sink is clogged, it's
    time to call diploma.**

Knock-knock.
  Who's there?
Gladys.
  Gladys who?
Gladys see you.

Knock-knock.
  Who's there?
Juan.
  Juan who?
Juan of your brothers.

Knock-knock.
  Who's there?
Norway.
  Norway who?
Norway will I wait for you!

Knock-knock.
  Who's there?
America.
  America who?
'Am Erica. Who are you?

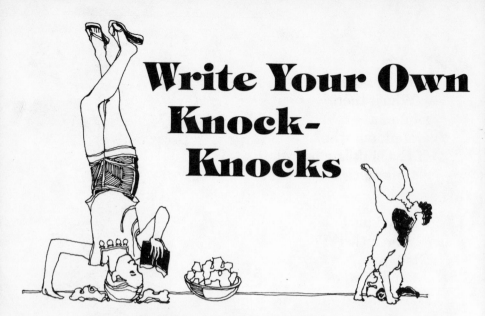

Write Your Own Knock-Knocks

Some things are nearly impossible to resist: not eating potato chips when everyone around you is emptying the bowl; yawning when someone you're talking to begins to yawn; saying, "Who's there?" whenever someone says, "Knock-knock."

Like most of the wisecracks we chuckle over, knock-knock jokes make use of a formula—a special way of telling the joke that makes it what it is. The teller adds a clever answer and then a punch line to a basic formula. The formula includes: "Knock-knock"; "who's there?" and a repetition of the answer in question form.

Example (the formula parts are in italics):
Knock-knock.
   Who's there?
Arthur.
   Arthur who?
Arthur any potato chips left in the bowl?

The answer to a knock-knock joke is often a humorous misuse of a word based on the way the word sounds. It is like a pun in that it is a play on words; it plays on the similar sound of different words.

For example:

Knock-knock.
   Who's there?
Amos.
   Amos who?
A mosquito bit me.

Knock-knock.
   Who's there?
Andy.
   Andy who?
Andy bit me again.

You can tell by the two often-told jokes above that to think up your own knock-knock jokes you have to listen carefully to a word and think about how it sounds and what other words sound similar. The examples here will help you catch the idea.

Rhoda: rode a

Dewey: do we

Butternut: better not

Thistle: this will

Ken: can

Phil: fill

Lettuce: let us

Betty: bet he

19

Once you have an idea for an answer and an idea for the words which sound like the answer, you are ready to write a silly saying to finish your joke. For example:

(Thistle) Thistle be a barrel of fun.
(Ken) Ken you do it?
(Lettuce) Lettuce begin.

Say each word in the list below and think about what word or words sound like it. On a separate piece of paper write down the ones you like best. (Those will be the words you use to begin writing your own silly sayings to answer your own knock-knock jokes.)

ears	hill	Puffin
unaware	Popeye	scold

Rita	needle	Siam	Boo
pizza	Luke	market	police
Mandy	June	Ben	Heidi
cashew	Sawyer	offer	

Once you have your list finished, go back over it and write a silly saying to go with each answer. To make your joke truly a knock-knock joke, remember to use the formula:

Knock-knock.
 Who's there?
XXXXXXXXXXXXXXXXXX*
 XXXXXXXXXXXXXXXX who?
XXXXXXXXXXXXXXXXXXXXXXXXXXX

*Only you can tell what this joke is because you have to write it before you can read it!

Write as many knock-knocks as you can. Then when someone asks you something like the joke below, knock 'em out with your very own knock-knocks!

Knock-knock.
 Who's there?
Genoa.
 Genoa who?
Genoa new knock-knock joke?

Laughable, Lovable, Limericks

This chapter is full of limericks—funny five line sayings that rhyme. The first two lines are long. The second two are short. The last line is long again.

Here's an example:

> A tutor who tooted a flute
> Tried to tutor two tooters to toot.
>   Said the two to the tutor,
>   "Is it harder to toot, or
> To tutor two tooters to toot?"
>   —ANONYMOUS

A man named Edward Lear made limericks popular. Lear began writing limericks way back in the 1800s. He wrote the funny sayings to amuse the grandchildren of his friends. Ever since then, people have been laughing at limericks. Here are some for you to laugh at, too!

There Was a Young Lady Whose Chin

There was a young lady whose chin
Resembled the point of a pin;
  So she had it made sharp,
  And purchased a harp,
And played several tunes with her chin.
             —EDWARD LEAR

A Diner at Crewe

A diner while dining at Crewe
Found quite a large mouse in his stew.
  Said the waiter, "Don't shout,
  And wave it about,
Or the rest will be wanting one, too."
             —ANONYMOUS

The Ice-Skating Miss

There was once a most charming young miss
Who considered her ice-skating bliss;
   But one day, alack!
   Her skates, they were slack,
And she ended up something like this.
      —ANONYMOUS

The Wright Boy

Said a boy to his teacher one day:
"Wright has not written rite right, I say."
   And the teacher replied,
   As the blunder she eyed:—
"Right!—Wright, write rite right, right away!"
      —ANONYMOUS

A Young Farmer

There was a young farmer of Leeds,
Who swallowed six packets of seeds.
   It soon came to pass
   He was covered with grass,
And he couldn't sit down for the weeds.
      —ANONYMOUS

The Mouse

A mouse in her room woke Miss Dowd;
She was frightened and screamed very loud.
   Then a happy thought hit her—
   To scare off the critter,
She sat up in bed and meowed.
               —ANONYMOUS

Two Cats of Kilkenny

There once were two cats of Kilkenny;
Each thought there was one cat too many;
   So they fought and they fit,
   And they scratched and they bit,
Till instead of two cats there weren't any.
               —ANONYMOUS

Hurtful Habits

There was an old person whose habits
Induced him to feed upon rabbits;
   When he'd eaten eighteen,
   He turned perfectly green,
Upon which he relinquished those habits.
               —EDWARD LEAR

An Old Man from Peru

There was an old man from Peru,
Who dreamed he was eating his shoe.
   He awoke in the night
   And turned on the light
And found it was perfectly true.
             —ANONYMOUS

An Old Person of Prague

There was an Old Person of Prague,
Who was suddenly seized with the plague;
   But they gave him some butter,
   Which caused him to mutter.
And cured that Old Person of Prague.
           —EDWARD LEAR

The Sultan

The Sultan got sore at his harem
And invented a scheme for to scare 'em;
   He caught him a mouse
   Which he loosed in the house;
(The confusion is called harem-scarem).
           —ANONYMOUS

A Cheerful Old Bear

A cheerful old bear at the zoo
Could always find something to do.
  When it bored him to go
  On a walk to and fro,
He reversed it, and walked fro and to.
—ANONYMOUS

A Young Fellow of Perth

There was a young fellow of Perth,
Who was born on the day of his birth;
  He was married, they say,
  On his wife's wedding day,
And he died when he quitted the earth.
—ANONYMOUS

A Young Man of Herne Bay

There was a young man of Herne Bay
Who was making explosives one day;
  But he dropped his cigar
  In the gunpowder jar.
There *was* a young man of Herne Bay.
—ANONYMOUS

27

A Man of Bengal

There was a young man of Bengal,
Who went to a fancy dress ball;
   He went, just for fun,
   Dressed up as a bun,
And a dog ate him up in the hall.
            —ANONYMOUS

An Old Person of Dean

There was an old person of Dean,
Who dined on one pea and one bean;
   For he said, "More than that
   Would make me too fat,"
That cautious old person of Dean.
            —EDWARD LEAR

An Old Lady of Rye

There was an old lady of Rye,
Who was baked by mistake in a pie;
   To the household's disgust
   She emerged through the crust,
And exclaimed, with a yawn, "Where am I?"
            —ANONYMOUS

The Old Man of the Hague

There was an old man of the Hague,
Whose ideas were excessively vague;
  He built a balloon
  To examine the moon,
That deluded old man of the Hague.
           —EDWARD LEAR

A Young Lady of Ealing

There was a young lady of Ealing,
Who had a peculiar feeling
  That she was a fly,
  And wanted to try
To walk upside down on the ceiling.
           —ANONYMOUS

Robbie

A certain young gallant named Robbie
Rode his steed back and forth in the lobby;
  When they told him, "Indoors
  Is no place for a horse,"
He replied, "Well, you see, it's my hobby."
        —ANONYMOUS

The Bottle of Perfume

The bottle of perfume that Willie sent
Was highly displeasing to Millicent;
  Her thanks were so cold
  They quarreled, I'm told,
Through that silly scent Willie sent Millicent.
        —ANONYMOUS

A Young Man from Elnora

There was a young man from Elnora
Who married a girl called Lenora.
  But he had not been wed
  Very long, 'til he said:
"Oh, drat it! I've married a snorer."
        —ANONYMOUS

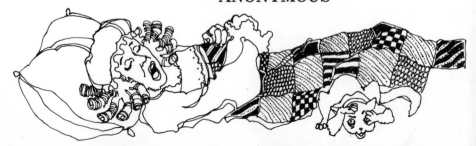

The Man in the Kettle

There was an old man who when little
Fell casually into a kettle;
   But, growing too stout,
   He could never get out,
So he passed all his life in that kettle.
          —ANONYMOUS

A Young Lady's Nose

There is a young lady whose nose
Continually prospers and grows;
   When it grew out of sight,
   She exclaimed in a fright,
"Oh! Farewell to the end of my nose!"
          —EDWARD LEAR

The Lady and the Thief

There was an old lady who said,
When she found a thief under her bed,
   "Get up from the floor;
   You're too close to the door,
And I fear you'll take cold in your head."
          —ANONYMOUS

AH-AH-AAH-AH

A Man of West Dumpet

There was an old man of West Dumpet
Who possessed a large nose like a trumpet;
   When he blew it aloud,
   It astonished the crowd,
And was heard through the whole of West Dumpet.
          —EDWARD LEAR

Lucy

His sister, named Lucy O'Finner,
Grew constantly thinner and thinner,
   The reason was plain—
   She slept out in the rain,
And was never allowed any dinner.
          —LEWIS CARROLL

An Old Man With a Beard

There was an old man with a beard,
Who said, "It's just as I feared!—
   Two owls and a hen,
   Four larks and a wren,
Have all built their nests in my beard!"
          —EDWARD LEAR

False Teeth

There was an old man of Black Heath,
Who sat on his set of false teeth;
  Said he, with a start,
  "O Lord, bless my heart!
I've bitten myself underneath!"
                    —ANONYMOUS

A Lady of Brooking

There was an old lady of Brooking,
Who had a great genius for cooking;
  She could bake sixty pies
  All quite the same size,
And tell which was which without looking.
                    —ANONYMOUS

An Old Person of Rhodes

There was an Old Person of Rhodes,
Who strongly objected to toads;
  He paid several cousins
  To catch them by dozens,
That futile Old Person of Rhodes.
                    —EDWARD LEAR

Now It's Your Turn

Now that you've read many famous limericks, how about *writing* some of those funny sayings.

You've probably noticed that many limericks begin with a line like this:

"There was a/an _____ from _____.

(PERSON—old man, old woman, young man, young woman, etc.)

(PLACE—city, town, country, etc.)

To begin your own limerick, write the above line, filling in the blanks with the words of your choice. Carefully choose the place—city, town, or country, etc. (You'll need to find a word that rhymes with the place for the word at the end of the second line.)

Like this:

There was a *young girl* from *Hale.*

Next, add a line that describes something about the person. For example:

> There was a young girl from Hale,
> *Who discovered her dog had no tail.*

Then, write two more lines (shorter ones this time) that further explain something about the person. And choose words for the end of the two lines that rhyme with each other. (See below.)

> There was a young girl from Hale,
> Who discovered her dog had no tail.
> *She said with a cry,*
> *"Oh no, what have I?"*

Finally, add the last line. It should rhyme with the last word used in the first two lines.

> There was a young girl from Hale,
> Who discovered her dog had no tail.
> She said with a cry,
> "Oh no, what have I?"
> *Then she got out a hammer and nail.*

35

Of course, limericks don't have to start out by naming a person and a place. Some limericks simply begin by telling about a funny or silly situation. For example:

Say, did you hear of the baboon
Who was in love with a raccoon?

You'll notice that the rhyme scheme is always the same, no matter how the limerick starts out. That is, the first two lines rhyme together, the second two lines rhyme with each other, and the last (fifth) line rhymes with the first two lines. Like this:

Say, did you hear of the baboon
Who was in love with a raccoon?
   They married one day
   In a little cafe.
Then they left for a trip to the moon!

You can write limericks about anything! Just think up funny things about people, places, events, animals, etc. Then all you have to do is remember the rhyme scheme.

Let's write some limericks together!

Say there was an old man from somewhere,
Who went riding one day on his mare.
  Tell what happened to him—
  Why he went for a swim,
And why he came up for air while still bare!

How about writing a limerick about a favorite teacher? Such as this:

I remember a teacher named Ms. Peel,
Who looked very much like a seal.
  But her heart was pure gold—
  That's what I was told . . .
So I sold her, and made a good deal!

*****

Don't give up writing limericks too early,
Even though they may make your hair curly.
  They're really much fun
  That is—when they're done . . .
So remember, don't give up on them early!

Other Silly Sayings

Many of the silly sayings we laugh at today have been told over and over for years and years. They are part of what is called oral tradition. That is, sayings and stories that one generation tells the next generation . . . and on and on.

Here are some examples of silly stories, poems, and other things that have been passed on to us from generations of long ago.

Two friends were talking.
    Kevin: Will you remember me in 20 years?
    Jan: Yes, of course I will.
    Kevin: Will you remember me in 15 years?
    Jan: Yes.
    Kevin: Will you remember me in 10 years?
    Jan: You know I will.
    Kevin: Will you remember me in five years?
    Jan: Yes.
    Kevin: Will you remember me in two years?
    Jan: Yes, why do you ask?
    Kevin: Will you remember me in one year?
    Jan: Yes.
    Kevin: Knock-knock.
    Jan: Who's there?
    Kevin: See! You forgot me already.

I Eat My Peas With Honey

I eat my peas with honey;
I've done it all my life.
It makes the peas taste funny,
But it keeps them on the knife.

* * *

Did you hear about old Mr. Hightower who lived on the hill? Before he died he asked that he be given a very grand funeral. His relatives decided to buy him the finest casket available and have it carried to the hilltop cemetery in a white cart drawn by a white horse.

Part way up the hill a rabbit hopped out of the bush and spooked the horse. It reared and jerked the cart so hard that the coffin slipped off and slid down the road.

It slid down the hill and into the town. It slid into the drugstore, down the aisle, and smacked into the pharmacy counter. The pharmacist was speechless. The lid popped open; Mr. Hightower sat up and said, "Do you have anything to stop this coffin?"

Why Fire Engines Are Red

Fire engines are red.
Newspapers are read, too.
Two and two make four.
Three times four equal twelve.
There are twelve inches in a foot.
A foot is also a ruler.
Queen Mary was a ruler.
Queen Mary was also a ship.
Ships sail on the ocean.
Fish swim in the ocean.
Fish have fins.
The Finns fought the Russians.
Russians are red.
Fire engines are always a-rushin'.
That's why fire engines are red.

I Often Pause and Wonder

I often pause and wonder
　At fate's peculiar ways,
For nearly all our famous men
　Were born on holidays.

Get a friend to help you tell a story. Have your friend say "just like me" after each phrase you say. (See below).

I went up on the porch and opened the door.
Just like me.
I went inside and climbed up one flight of stairs.
Just like me.
I climbed up two flights of stairs.
Just like me.
I walked down a long, dark hall.
Just like me.
I went into a big room.
Just like me.
I walked over to a dresser and looked in a mirror.
Just like me.
I saw a monkey.
Just like me.
Just like you?

The Train Pulled in the Station

O, the train pulled in the station,
   The bell was ringing wet;
The track ran by the depot,
   And I think it's running yet.

'Twas midnight on the ocean,
   Not a streetcar was in sight;
The sun and moon were shining,
   And it rained all day that night.

'Twas a summer day in winter,
   And the snow was raining fast;
As a barefoot boy, with shoes on,
   Stood, sitting on the grass.

O, I jumped into the river
   Just because it had a bed;
I took a sheet of water
   For to cover up my head.

O, the rain makes all things beautiful,
   The flowers and grasses, too;
If the rain makes all things beautiful,
   I wish it would rain on you!

               —AMERICAN
               FOLK SONG

BOUND FOR BOMBAY

There Was a Young Lady Residing at Prague

There was a young lady residing at Prague,
Whose ideas were really most wonderfully vague.
When anyone said to her: "What a fine day!"
"Roast chicken is nice," she would dreamily say,
"And a mushroom on toast is the very best thing
To make a canary or hummingbird sing."
The people of Prague thought this conduct so
    strange,
They quickly decided she needed a change,
So they packed her with care in a box with some
    hay,
And paid her expenses as far as Bombay.

Old Hogan's Goat

Old Hogan's goat was feeling fine,
Ate six red shirts off the line;
Old Hogan grabbed him by the back
And tied him to the railroad track.
Now when the train came into sight,
That goat grew pale and green with fright;
He heaved a sigh, as if in pain,
Coughed up those shirts and flagged the train!

Some Epitaphs

Here lies John Knott;
His father was Knott before him.
He lived Knott, died Knott,
Yet underneath his stone doth lie
Knott christened, Knott begot,
And here he lies and still is Knott.

A zealous locksmith died of late
And did arrive at the pearly gate.
He stood without and would not knock,
Because he planned to pick the lock.

Beneath this stone a lump of clay
Lies Uncle Peter Daniels,
Who too early in the month of May
Took off his winter flannels.

Jump Rope Rhymes

Johnny over the ocean; Johnny over the sea.
Johnny broke a pop bottle and blamed it onto me.
How many whippings will I get?
   1, 2, 3, 4, etc.

Order in the court,
The judge is eating beans.
His wife is in the bathtub
Counting submarines.
How many did she count?
   1, 2, 3, 4, etc.

Teddy bear, teddy bear, turn around.
Teddy bear, teddy bear, touch the ground.
Teddy bear, teddy bear, climb the stairs.
Teddy bear, teddy bear, say your prayers.
Teddy bear, teddy bear, turn off the light.
Teddy bear, teddy bear, say good-night.
Teddy bear, teddy bear, shine your shoes.
Teddy bear, teddy bear, now skidoo.

So no one can see, write the word "what" on a piece of paper and fold it up. Then say to a friend:

"I know what you're going to say next."

Friend: What?

Show him the paper and say, "See, I knew you would say that."

A Skunk Sat On A Stump

A skunk sat on a stump.
The skunk thinked
the stump stunk,
but the stump thunk
the skunk stunk.

Try this on a friend:
"Think of a number. Any number at all.
Now, add eight.
Got it? Okay. Subtract two.
Now, close your eyes."
(Wait until your friend's eyes are closed.)
"Dark, isn't it!"

ROUND-IN-A-CIRCLE STORIES

Has anyone ever told you a story that ended up right back where it started? Such a story is known as a circle story.

To write a circle story or song, you must start off with a line, keep adding to it, and then end up by repeating it. The story then goes on and on.

Round-in-a-circle stories are easy and fun to write. Here are some lines to help you start.

Last night I:

    Made a snowman . . .   Saw a circus . . .

    Met an orangutan . . .   Found a lemon . . .

    Climbed a mountain . . .

As an example, see the famous circle story below. It is often sung. Called "Found a Peanut," the words go like this:

Found a peanut, found a peanut,
Found a peanut just now.
Just now, I found a peanut.
Found a peanut just now.

I split it open, split it open,
Split it open just now.
Just now, I split it open.
Split it open just now.

Found it rotten, found it rotten,
Found it rotten just now.
Just now I found it rotten.
Found it rotten, just now.

I ate it anyway, ate it anyway,
Ate it anyway, just now.
Just now I ate it anyway,
Ate it anyway, just now.

Got a tummy-ache, got a tummy-ache,
Got a tummy-ache just now.
Just now I got a tummy-ache,
Got a tummy-ache just now.

Called my doctor, called my doctor,
Called my doctor, just now.
Just now I called my doctor,
Called my doctor, just now.

Feeling better, feeling better.
Feeling better just now.
Just now, I'm feeling better,
Feeling better just now.

Found a peanut, found a peanut,
Found a peanut, just now.
Just now I found a peanut,
Found
   a peanut
      just
         now. . . .